Spectral Realms

No. 21 ‡ Summer 2024

Edited by S. T. Joshi

> The spectral realms that thou canst see
> With eyes veil'd from the world and me.
>
> H. P. LOVECRAFT, "To a Dreamer"

SPECTRAL REALMS is published twice a year by Hippocampus Press,
P.O. Box 641, New York, NY 10156 (www.hippocampuspress.com).
Copyright © 2024 by Hippocampus Press.
All works are copyright © 2024 by their respective authors.
Cover art and design by Daniel V. Sauer
Hippocampus Press logo by Anastasia Damianakos.

ISBN 978-1-61498-448-1   ISSN 2333-4215

Contents

Poems 5

   Solstice Ghosts / Ann K. Schwader 7
   On Gustave Doré's Engraving *The Vision of Death* / Manuel Pérez-
      Campos 8
   Too Close to the Sun / Claire Smith 10
   Cronos, I Won't Bow to Thee / Andrew White 12
   The Withershades / Joshua Green 13
   At the End Was the Castle Someday / Maxwell I. Gold 14
   Together Always / Ngo Binh Anh Khoa 16
   In Praise of the Dreamer / Lauri Taneli Lassila 19
   Hungry Pumpkins / Katherine Kerestman 20
   A Lover's Little Lies / William Clunie 22
   Take You Away / Mary Turzillo 23
   We Are Becoming Demonic Machines / John Shirley 24
   Samhain House / Carl E. Reed 26
   The Sea Hag / Chelsea Arrington 27
   The Explanation of the Mystery / Frank Coffman 28
   Screams from the Pit / David Barker 31
   Infernal Candle / Scott J. Couturier 32
   Hero Redux / Melissa Ridley Elmes 34
   The Owlmoot / Adam Bolivar 36
   The Widow's Room / Steven Withrow 37
   Churchyard Nuncheon / Manuel Arenas 38
   Dark Window / Denise Dumars 40
   Earth Shall Be Ours Again / Manuel Pérez-Campos 41
   Purity / John Thomas Allen 42
   Song for the Devouring One / Dmitri Akers 44
   If Closets Talked / Maxwell I. Gold 47
   Take Out / Jay Hardy 48
   Cassilda's Song / DJ Tyrer 50
   What Evil Lurks / Adele Gardner 51
   Andrea in Wonderland / Andrew White 52
   Changing Moons / Oliver Smith 54
   Rabbit Led / Ashley Dioses 56

Lovemaking / Michael Potts 58
What Do We Believe? / Darrell Schweitzer 59
Vestibule of Tomorrow / Adam Amberden.......................................60
Conundrum / Janice Klain 62
Vision of Ys / Wade German 63
Rising Star / David C. Kopaska-Merkel 64
Venom / Arukoya Tamois 65
The Path / G. O. Clark...66
The Dark Seasons / Geoffrey Reiter..68
Cemetery Dansers / Katherine Kerestman..69
For the *Weird Tales* Poets / Steven Withrow 70
The Dying Flower of My Soul / Scott J. Couturier...........................71
Gossamer Gateways / Frank Coffman 72
Sor Maria and the Devil, Luzbel / Manuel Arenas 73
A Pestilence of Tongues / Joshua Green..74
The Old Gray Mansion / Ngo Binh Anh Khoa................................75
Dead Summer / Denise Dumars 76
The Messengers / Manuel Pérez-Campos..77
Warm Fall / Don Webb..78
The Stench That Lingers Still / Ngo Binh Anh Khoa.....................79
Sirens / Marge Simon and Mary Turzillo..80
The Trumpets / Maxwell I. Gold 82
The Old Fisherman / Joy Yin 83
Mocking Delight / DJ Tyrer..84
A Moonlit Pursuit / Joshua Gage 86
During Happy Hour at the Undead Lounge / LindaAnn LoSchiavo.... 87
A Highland Cairn / Josh Maybrook..88
On the Strings of Fear / Norbert Góra 89
Comes the Reaper / Lori R. Lopez...90
The Starveling Girl / Steven Withrow 92
When the Dead Dance with Us / Darrell Schweitzer......................94
Who Knows the End? / Geoffrey Reiter 95
Dr. Frankenstein's Witch-Princess / Arukoya Tomais....................96
Autumn / Scott J. Couturier 98

    Born Again / Frank Coffman 99
    The Hall Between Labyrinths / Joshua Green 100
Classic Reprints **101**
    The Were-Wolves / William Wilfred Campbell 103
    The Other Side of a Mirror / Mary Elizabeth Coleridge 107
Reviews **109**
    The "Wyrd" Tradition / Leigh Blackmore 111
    Cats, Death, and Poetry / S. T. Joshi 113
    The Poetry of Youth / Leigh Blackmore 116
Notes on Contributors **118**

From the Editor: In *Spectral Realms* No. 20, the last five lines of Lori R. Lopez's "Ravensong" appear on p. 95, through typesetting error, as the ending for "Of Shapeshifters Spawned by the Revolution" by Manuel Pérez-Campos.

Poems

Solstice Ghosts

Ann K. Schwader

This longest night awakens those who wait
along the margins of our hearts until
last sunlight gutters out. Why hesitate
at invitation? Shadows gather still
& thick at every window to fulfill
lost Samhain's vanished promise. Let that veil
between attenuate before the will—
no, longing—to be haunted. Let some pale
& insufficient moon begin its tale
of memory, thin crescent cutting deep
until blood comes. Until the past prevails
as some last candle-end is found to keep
faith with these lingerers beyond, & spark
a beacon flame that calls them from the dark.

On Gustave Doré's Engraving *The Vision of Death*

Manuel Pérez-Campos

> And I looked, and beheld a pale horse: and his name that sat on him was Death, and hell followed with him. And power was given unto them over the fourth part of the earth. . . . —Revelation 6:7–8, KJV

Enwrapped in a buffeted swirl of long cape,
His forehead suffused by the glow of a red star,
the fourth semi-invisible progeny of the opened seals,
an archangel of enticing aspect and face raptured
by the dark power vested in Him to render the actual un-possible
rides on a superheated road of air out of a cloudy gateway
to the bottomless pit impossibly erect,
commanding a mauler steed of frightful frictionless eminence
while followed several mountains away
by a vortexlike bevy of winged subaltern demons
and all that His shadow touches fleetingly as he passes over it
seems to Him alien and unfamiliar.

He cackles
at peasants of broad-brimmed hat and long sleeved shirt
who perceived through his brutal, daring temperament
seem apparitions scampering to reach a deciduous hideout or a holy
    place
and veering away lowers incuriously as though through afterthought
His ponderous scythe: and as the silver cord within each is severed

they drop suddenly in mid-race, their souls released from that chamber
    of horrors
which their crumpled forms scattered on a narrow strip that escaped
    reaping
shall soon become, doomed to wander the earth
until it dissolves into space and their souls with it.

And as we, the mournfully attired procession in pointed hats and
    glittering crowns—having poured out of the drawbridge from our
    nine-towered castle—
stand on a high lea in a wide circle to bid ritual farewell to one another,
an ice-mist slithers away cumbrously from a nearby weed-strangled stream
and encircles us like a serpent building supercilious coils unendingly such
that whoso is opposite one seems diminutive and by the next high-
    sounding
orison we do not see who it is we are truly holding hands with:
and then our subminds like a sibyl's are infused greatly with vision
until we see the unconsummated madness of the centuries
that He shall abide among us as regent coming swiftly toward us.

Too Close to the Sun

Claire Smith

says that if he wants a pair of wings he has nothing to do but to pray to God &
*he will get them**

What do you find
when you try to take off and fly
from the asylum's roof-top?

To grow wings, to fly over rose-beds,
walled gardens; to soar free, past
iron-gates over fields, villages, towns
away from this place. You with wings

feathers across your back
held on by wax. As if a candle's
light shows your path, leads
you through the maze
to safety, back home.

*Gloucester, Gloucestershire Archives (GA), Item Reference Unknown, Bodily Health and Condition of Jo— St——, in Notice of Admission, written by Edmund L. Rowe, Medical Officer of City and County of Gloucester Pauper Lunatic Asylum, in Wotton near Gloucester, 18 September 1885.

You've been warned you will lose
your wings if you veer too close
to the sun, plummet into the ocean,
beyond help, drowned.

This time the Gods
are deaf to your prayers,
just an embrace from the ground.

Cronos, I Won't Bow to Thee

Andrew White

Prelude

I must break the back of time,
End its tyrannical rule
Over my state of mind.
Then I will be purged
Of an inglorious burden—
No longer restless
Or craving what comes next.

Rising

Cronos, I won't bow to thee;
I'll rise above, I will be free.
A thousand days shall be as none
When the battle has been won.

Apotheosis

The clock is moving,
But time doesn't pass—
Its power has been broken.
I float through cloudless skies,
The cell beneath me empty.

The Withershades

Joshua Green

I tripped upon a fallen bough, within
A darkling wood of moving specters. Down
I looked in fear of being found, my skin
Adorned in gems of well-made dread. My crown
Then felt the touch of dirt, as roots made brown
Were lifted far above my head. Tangled
Strands of moonlit umbrage threatened to drown
My sight in withering souls entangled.
Withershades are made from bodies mangled,
So I saw that night—as they strode away.
Though they're blind they've used their hair and strangled
Visitors that stumble upon my way.

But now my house stands in a field bereft
E'er since the withershades have gone and left.

At the End Was the Castle Someday

Maxwell I. Gold

Where the tired exuberance that was a brilliant and belabored horizon, dragged towards infinity, I saw the terrible Castle Someday. High and proud was its architecture, with towers hewn from marble, granite, and bones of desperate, lonely men, who thought themselves masters of the inevitable, and inscrutable structures that climbed inexorably toward the unsettling skies; whose stars danced above as if to taunt the onlookers that something was coming. Bloated apertures gave caution for those who dared to enter the Castle where crooked mirrors and rusty pieces of ancient armor from a nameless forgotten civilization lined the old carpets along a series of demented Gaudian corridors, which weaved in and out like some grotesque, labyrinthine queasiness. The scent of metal and burnt wax filled the stone halls, mixing with a viridescent spectral glow.

There were few who knew the truth of the Castle Someday and its dreadful existence. Deep inside, secrets of the impossibility of stars swirled within pits far below, languishing in chains long since thought to have perished to Time's lugubrious song.

Concealed in the strangest, most unsettling basements beneath the dust and derisive thoughts that pressed o'er the endless ages as if fat and heinous digits; prepared to asphyxiate a single voice—the last possibility twitched in silent shadows, calling from a crooked dungeon, *I am the end.*

The last note, a string pulled in the lowly dark whereupon its soft and lonely tone hung in the deep, sad recesses of the night—*I am the end.* Concealed no longer, the foundations of that ancient castle gave way, jubilantly, to its immutable destruction where the tired exuberance that was a brilliant and belabored horizon crumbled against infinity, and I saw at the end of everything, the terrible Castle Someday.

Together Always

Ngo Binh Anh Khoa

"We'll be together always,"
My mother says to me
Before her last breath leaves her,
And silenced hence is she.

I feel the moment her soul
Becomes an autumn breeze;
Her mortal flesh grows colder
Once her faint heartbeats cease.

But I reject what Fate's dealt—
To be alive alone,
Deprived of mother's touches,
The warmth of my life gone.

Rage wages war with mourning
To take revenge for her.
Sheer hatred flows with my tears;
The dark blood in me stirs—

The blood that I am cursed with
Through my unholy birth,
Whose seal, once wavering, shatters.
It yearns to scorch the Earth.

I sense the air grow heavy,
I feel the forest quake,
I hear the wind turn vicious
And watch the Heavens shake.

I feel as though I'm burning
As magic overflows
From out my shivering being,
Which spreads out and explodes.

And from the ground there rumbling,
A million souls arise—
Of fiends and beasts and humans;
Resounding are their cries.

Before my ruined shelter,
They all in reverence kneel,
All waiting for my order
As light to darkness yields.

Among them is my mother,
A ghost transparent, gray,
Who joins me where I'm panting,
And by my side she'd stay.

Though we are now of two worlds,
We are a family still—
Forevermore and always;
Damn what the Heavens will!

We chose to live as hermits;
We chose to harm no one,
But man still hunts and hurts us.
They'll pay for what they've done!

We chose peace over violence,
But they won't leave us be.
Their fear, thus, shall be realized:
A Demon King they'll see!

In Praise of the Dreamer

Lauri Taneli Lassila

vessels of dark light
stream across the blackened sky
harken back, augurs, to ends long ago begun
to the death the dying of which is underway
under an abyss of sleep & thunder & molten clay

dreams which project across the seas of stars
into undying lands of undying sleep, civilizational vistas
long ago taken over by starry grass and somic dreams

kings sleep there among their slaves
deaf to our calls, deaf to all
but the dreams of the undying dreamer
who sleeps at the bottom of all seas & all dreams

death to all but he who sleeps the undying dream!

Hungry Pumpkins

Katherine Kerestman

Bloated like corpses' lips, pumpkin seeds bulge,
Brast ope their seams—and from them tendrils creep,
Escape their shells to morbid tastes indulge,
Disinter fields to ghastly repasts reap.

"My little lad—where is he?" anguished, cries
A distraught dame. Her errant child lost
In fields of pumpkins, searching for his prize,
Resolved to choose a pumpkin, too engrossed
In dreams of burning Jack-o'-Lantern eyes.
He'd called his mum, but she'd failed to hear him.
He'd tried to lift the biggest one in size.
He'd tried to stretch his arms about its rim
When, shuddering, the pumpkin pulled *him* in,
Dragged him, headlong, through cold, wet, furrowed loam,
Thick vines entwined about his arms and shins,
Pulled him into the chasm of the Gnome,

Below the earth. Twelve slaves planting pumpkins—
Two dozen arms stretched high above their heads,
Straining to the rafters—seizing bumpkins—
Captured souls obliged to sow pumpkin beds,
Succulent vineyards, glistening orange spheres
That beguile wand'ring townsfolk, tempting some
To turn off the road, set aside their fears,
Carry a gay cornucopia home.

When pumpkins' slaves give out from overwork
Their eyeballs are torn from out their faces,
To goggle from Jack-o'-Lanterns' cutwork,
Erstwhile friends' last enduring traces.

Mind you, keep clear of pumpkin patches, too,
Or live your life enslaved in pumpkin-land,
Forever planting pumpkins from below,
Setting pumpkin snares for human viands.

A Lover's Little Lies

William Clunie

I found a musty grimoire
in the armoire of Eileen,
the grandmother of my lover.

I made a gross mistake
in opening that fusty book
and casually intoning random verse.

And now I see my lover as she is,
a withered ancient with a gift
for hypnotizing fools like me.

Take You Away

Mary Turzillo

We won't need your ponies,
Your fey desperadoes,
Your born-again wolfmen,
Your church wraiths and shades.
Don't you know I'm the West Wind
    and I flew here to blow you away.

You can leave all your hot lead,
Your dream-gems, book magic,
Your printer's cap, radar,
Your CIA meter or wheel.
Don't you know I'm your dark side,
    And I'll sweetly shanghai you away.

I don't need your mirrors
or haunted projector,
I'll give them all back to you,
give them away.
Don't you know I'm your Hecate,
    and I've tripped here to witch you away.

You can pack up your basket
of counterfeit pot shards,
your dead copper keys and balloons.
Don't you know? I'm your Princess
    and I've come here to take you away.

We Are Becoming Demonic Machines

John Shirley

Neuroses
etch into the brain;
Full doses
Of illumined pain—
Patterns repeat,
Become a stain

And soon we are
rapacious machines,
Programmed by repetition;
From the passive aggressive
To the truly obscene—
We are becoming demonic machines

Demons who gnaw through
The biospheric skin of Earth;
Who swarm like locusts
Despoiling
The paradise of our birth—

We form them inside,
Imprint by imprint,
One engraving at a time:

Day by angry, fearful day
Decisions coated in grime—

We are becoming demonic machines

Cyborgs scurry from the light
Of consciousness
Demons who blither
In the sight of consciousness

Who hide in shadows
that pool within—
Fattened with circuits
As our souls shrink thin

We are
becoming
Demonic
Machines.

Samhain House

Carl E. Reed

The house at the end of the ville isn't there;
    it fades in & out like the fog
that rolls in clouds of gray-misted swirls
    from out the enveloping bog.

Worm-rotted timbers & thatched-grass roof
    went up in pre-Roman Gaul;
burnt to the ground long centuries past
    it returns Samhain Eve to appall.

Beware its tenebrous, shifting form—
    not home but a monstrous mouth;
cross its threshold to bottomless void—
    lighten, thin . . . wink out!

The Sea Hag

Chelsea Arrington

Ribbons of sandy seaweed writhe in my matted
locks of bracken-gray & black. Seashells clank like discordant
bells as I raise my arms to the monstrous moon,
and whistle up the wind, winding the weather
'round my bony fingers & wrists: casting
it out to do my will of wreck & ruin.
Swaying & screaming, I dance: my barren breasts
naked under the starless sky as I invoke
drowned gods with my cursed words.
When sailors & seals drift a-shore, bloated, & blue
with sightless eyes, I open them with my shale dagger
and coax sooth & portents from the entrails and bile
of Mannanán's unwilling sacrifices.
Laughter & cackles vomit from my putrid mouth
as images of maidens' murders & cuckolded kings
take shape before my watery eyes.
Monasteries aflame, pillage & rapine
Twist in the reeking death before me.
My salted lips smack and a wordless song escapes:
sounds of cracking bones & surf.
When I have done, my only friends, fiendish gulls
lay gasping fishies at my feet. Raw & bloody,
I swallow them & once sated, return to my lonely cave
where I sleep & dream of the swelling, deep, dark sea.

The Explanation of the Mystery

Frank Coffman

I. The Challenge

The day's long hike was over and the tent
Kept the outside cold to a bearable chill.
Without, the wind was wild, would not relent,
"Safe enough," they thought, at the base of that small hill.
"Let's each tell a scary story," one had said.
"I like that plan," the oldest one spoke out.
"I know a tale will fill you all with dread."
The rest just smiled and shook their heads in doubt.
"I swear it's true. I know a spell to evoke
An eldritch mystery, A tale few living know.
I'll warn you first—these words I never spoke."
The wind began to howl, a spray of snow
Blew in past tent flaps sealed against the night.
The listeners felt the first slight twinge of fright.

II. The Summoning

"Few know that there are Old Ones from the Void.
From the more-than-distant cosmos they have traveled
And will not rest 'til our world is destroyed,
Till our thought-to-be Reality is unravelled.

And I know a chant to open wide a door
To let them enter here—into our plane!
But, once open, I know not what horrors will pour
In through that gate!"
                        "Are you insane,"
A fellow tentmate asked, "to think we'd buy
This crazed suggestion that you have such power?
But the tale's a good one. Give your 'chant' a try!"
"I will! And you shall see—within the hour!"
The teller said. "Ngh'aaaa . . . Ngh'aaaa . . . h'yuh!
Yog-Sothoth . . . ygnaiih!" Wilder the wind blew!

III. The Arrival

His listeners were awed by his changing facial features,
As he intoned words no ears should ever hear!
Soon—what seemed to be the howls and grunts of creatures
Drowned out the moaning wind! They seemed quite near!
In terror, they cut small flaps in the canvas walls
To peer outside to see what moved about.
Meanwhile, the chants grew louder, as did the calls
From Beyond! One screamed "Out! We must get out!"

"Tear out the back," another said. "Run! Run!"
With knives they slashed the tent's wall open wide
And poured out, shoeless, to the deadly cold.

None of the nine would see another sun.
In terror they fled, but there was no place to hide
From things no Reason—no sane mind—can hold!

IV. The Discovery

They found some two weeks later. Very weird—
The stockinged, barefoot, one-shoed set of tracks,
Led to the scattered bodies of the first five,
Faces frozen, gazing at some Horror abjectly feared.
Two full months later the snowmelt brought climax—
Though it was clear that no one could survive—
But missing eyeballs, one victim's lips, a tongue,
A shattered skull and crushing of the chest,
Eyebrows burnt off—gruesome deaths of those so young.
The only satisfaction—they had found the rest.

But none of the first would-be "rescuers" at the scene,
Ever mentioned the finding of those curious trails
Of greenish slime. And imagination fails!
No words can describe those *tracks* that could not have been!

Screams from the Pit

David Barker

The farmer found a well that burrowed down
Quite far below the surface of his land
So deep it reached a bed of desert sand
Not native to the site the farm was found,
And with his son descended in the pit
To some mad realm where elder gods once walked.
Their story grew more odd, the more they talked.
They sealed it up; each other's throats they slit.

We laid the pair to rest then broke the seal
Upon the well and lowered down a crew
Intent on finding out how much was real
Of all the nonsense uttered by the two.
In darkness far below they clanked around:
Their violent deaths—God, what an awful sound!

Inspired by H. P. Lovecraft's sonnet "XI. The Well"
in *Fungi from Yuggoth*.

Infernal Candle

Scott J. Couturier

It is said the secrets of the witches' sabbath
may lurk within a wicked candle's flame. . . .
Light it, & allow the wick to wax
into bluish fires, shining arcane shibboleth.

Made from dead man's rotten tallow
plucked from gibbet's crow-pecked rope. . . .
Its glow casts forgotten words of hex,
sorcery to strike womb & orchard fallow.

Runes mar walls lit by yellow beams,
writ as if in runnels of blood. . . .
Spells wrought in fallen Lucifer's Hell,
revealed by a profane blaze which gleams.

Wiles of fell warlocks crowned in furze,
& witches whose wrath empyries razed. . . .
Wisdom of dust, of damnation's hot breath,
a lust to sell one's soul for Satan's spurs.

Kindle that candle come evening's fall,
& await eagerly legion shades of dusk. . . .
Scry the gloaming for learning infernal,
fraught by awe & dread sufficient to appall.

Then shall you glean archfiend's *geis*,
wield utterances to shudder pillars of Earth. . . .
Curses to cast down friend, foe, & firmament.
But at what price! You must burn, with no peace.

Hero Redux

Melissa Ridley Elmes

This is the hero's return—

What no one tells you is you have changed
irrevocably, and in that changing come to know
the world differently; when the dragon is slain,
the demon defeated, the horde turned back
and—tired, heartsore, all blisters and burns,
only wanting the comfort of a warm bath,
a cool cloth to the head, a pint of something malty
or a dram of something peaty and a hearth
at which to rest while those you've saved gather
round, happy to see you and welcome you home
battle-worn and victorious—you finally return
to find that nothing has changed but yourself.
Mother still nitpicks all your faults, gripes about
dusty footprints left on the clean carpet upon your
entrance, complains you've ruined your new shirt;
Father grumbles about thankless sons who forget
duty to go traipsing off on fool adventures, wasting
time and money in pursuits beyond their station;
Brother resents you've returned, staying his ascent
to favored heir; Sister disdains the beautiful gifts
you've brought her from far off lands: they are not
the latest fashion; and in your absence Beloved
has gone and betrothed herself to Frank, the farrier's

son, of all people, Frank, with his ruddy face and
lack of imagination. And there you are, a hero who
has saved them all and more besides—Dragonslayer,
Demon Hunter, Horde-Crusher, a man so much
the worse for wear, the better for experience, so much
what you've always wished to be and what they
should want—quietly going to your room amid their
complaints and jeers to take off those dirty clothes,
change into something respectable, brush your teeth,
comb your hair, and be down in time for dinner,
your head full of stories, your heart full of strength,
your spirit kicking and screaming again for escape,
your dreams haunting you, nightly revisitations
of a world you left behind, when you left this world
behind, and the man you were, are, could be

        —If only they would permit it.

The Owlmoot

Adam Bolivar

On Yule the owls   in an oak will roost,
A murky moot   in the moonlit night,
To quibble and quarrel   and classify wisdom,
Scribes and scholars,   skilled at cavil,
Their talons tearing   at the tiniest thread,
Unwinding the weave   of weak reason.
Born to their branches,   which bear the scores
Of far-off forebears   who founded the moot,
At the end of the night,   the owls scatter
To their lonely lives   of lore-poring,
Hunched in hiding   in the haunted wood.

The Widow's Room

Steven Withrow

The blanket, like a coffin lid,
Fit tight against the marriage bed
And lay there as her husband did,
But now the man was three weeks dead.

Impossibly she saw his shade
Resting where the mattress sagged,
Then caught herself and watched it fade,
His shirts and suits already bagged

To give away come morning. Still,
Her vision, be it ghost or not,
Had left her reeling with a chill.
Yet Harold's in his grave, she thought.

Kneeling for once, as though in prayer,
She chanted a faithless rosary:
There's no one there, there's nothing there.
(The blanket shook.) *It's only me . . .*

Churchyard Nuncheon

Manuel Arenas

Oh, won't you come to tea in the cemet'ry?
It will be oh so frightfully nice, you'll see.
We'll have buttered scones and black currant jelly,
And sundry sapid treats to bloat our bellies.
I've found a nice spot that's gloomily pleasant,
If you don't fancy sweets, I've also pheasant.
We can picnic on the slab of Mariah,
In potter's field, an unwanted pariah.
Do be careful as you walk past the headstones,
It would be ill-mannered to jounce the dead's bones.
And do so be quiet and use a light tread,
For it's not so wise to awaken the dead.
But come child, why do you still stand at the gate?
Come in straight away dear, do not hesitate.
Do you not, as do I, love dead folk my dear?
Pray come, let me teach you, you've nothing to fear.
The dead are docile if their sleep's undisturbed,
Tho' if they awaken, they will be perturbed.
Still, it's not the deceased whom you should fear,
It's Lucifer's cronies, that ever lurk near.
Maniacal ghouls who believe themselves beasts,
And dig up fresh graves for their carrion feasts.
Or Warlocks and Witches digging for prizes,
And baleful Lillim, in manifold guises.

But that's all at nightfall, and it is still day,
The sooner we finish, we'll be on our way.
To rest home by the fire, sipping mulled cider,
As the dead drowse with the worm and the spicer.

Dark Window

Denise Dumars

If the purpose of windows
is to see, what have we
to say about a dark window,
supernatural matter gone and done
with crushing glass and a mad dash
through the frame, Alice down
the rabbit hole, Neruda's
quiet-boned graves,
but coffins once had windows.
Imaging being buried,
screaming out
the small lozenge of glass
with no one to hear.
If we open the window
to the dark, what will rush in?
The dark is already here
and panes of glass
whether open or closed
cannot keep the dark out,
its energy eclipsing all that light.

Earth Shall Be Ours Again

Manuel Pérez-Campos

Anchored in the unrecorded gulfs before the advent
of ancestral memory an alluvion of all-penetrative
endlessly interanimated iterative trilobites have
overcrowded with varying degrees of dream solidity
a striated strip of chartreuse shale: here in lacunae-
riddled scenes where silence repeats itself is the tale
of their ad hoc phantom nations, striving to prosper with their pale
imprints an alternative to the anthropocene testament.

I, their secret worshipper, prop up with psychic energy a sunken
tribe of relicts that hides its transgressive shindig uncannily
under sludge and silt: they are able to wait ten million years: and when
earth at last turns into a heavy graveyard for humanity, they will
warble with current-borne abandon—their three-lobed symmetry
still invariant—and scrabble upward ever yonder in the deep dark chill.

Purity

John Thomas Allen

The dead are painless and abide in pure spirit.
They float, crucified, on Golgotha's matchsticks:
cubby whispers and punctured IV bags
baby hearts slowly beating war hymns.
Their faces suspend as orphaned moons,
nailed to oars, spun finely as Goldilocks'
braids to face their true stature, a thirsty soil
slaked by each man's sorrow.

Moonflowers blow in vacant sentries.
The reeds lit dimly with their gaslight,
and blow the pale wind song of consumption
Crucibles hold them steadfast on the River Styx,
Catherine's Wheel an ascetic sun satiated
with her salutary sign, the men's pores
sweating her menstruated grace in bottled
anodynes of salvific suffering, to echo
the widowed nursery rhymes,
a stripped melody of burning ogatwas.

I went back to Mass in winter.
The monstrance raised, filled with moon,
and found me in the back, a pair of eyes
rolling in the dark, I whispered that *even Lazarus*

would die, twice holy, filled with star light,
his chest rising in plague wheat, the weight
of joined arms in nodding mezzos.

The dead's eyes are loose and gentle, starry marrow
egg white and in shock, the growling hounds
in perpetual pause. Their bottled tears are a solvent
for sudden clowns, for a trickster god's embrace,
and the rain bled sloth of carnival dirges.

Song for the Devouring One

Dmitri Akers

The ropy litter thrash'd beneath the world,
With sable scales and claret underpart
As vilest worms emerged from viler heart
Inside the earthen darkness where they curl'd;
Their bloody bellies turn'd and nest unfurl'd.
And by the cavern's holes, as wounds that smart,
An altar stood—so carved for occult art—
With ancient symbols dreadful priests had whorl'd.

Upon the etching cover'd altar top
The ritual off'rings—blood and braided lock—
Had glow'd so azure on a horrid sign,
As croaking chorus rose and ne'er had stopp'd
For monstrous nestlings stirr'd against the rock:
Those summoned spawn had deigned to mock Design.

Within the cavern's shadow-mantled maw
The ruddy spawn was slith'ring out the dark,
Those serpent-whelps had never heard the lark,
Tho' groped toward the light with fang and claw.
Their sable eyes had leered at what they saw:
A magus held his wounds that bore the mark
Of wyrd, forgotten powers old and stark;
He groaned and crawled along the stony floor.

The wizened wizard—hurt and bleeding dry—
Had curs'd the birth of such a host of fiend,

The which had whined to be so timely weaned;
From deep within there came the brutal cry,
As worms had surged a raw deluge of rage
The which had fall'n upon the screaming mage.

Despite his caterwauling spells and prayer,
Things gorged upon the magus' toothsome head
And body till the nestling swarm had fed,
Tho' some had fattened much and burst: a blare
Of sanguine gore across the cavern lair.
The magick succour magi often bled
Had flourish'd them; the skins were shed
And ev'ry deadly serpent grew their share.

Those strength-infusèd things scraped 'cross the cave
And hissed as hungry stomachs went to roil,
The scaly serpent-daughters came to crave
The flesh and blood of men above the soil.
They writhed within the dark to deaf'ning shriek
And spill'd upon the world for souls to seek.

A stony city loomed within the dusk;
'Twas grain they milled from fruitful seeds they'd sown.
Along the wind a rotten stench was blown,
As murrains came to spoil and taint the husk,
For serpents stank as ancient, mummied musk,

A rot had risen from realms unknown.
They towered high above, as giants grown,
With lengthened fang, so long it seem'd a tusk.

With crying like the satyrs' pipes so loud,
They rampaged through laments for pain's reprieve;
The rev'lling horde began to rape and reave
Beneath a dark'ning sky and noxious cloud.
And all surviving prey were skinned for hide,
For serpents wore the skin as trophied pride!

Above, the moon had seethed to crimsons pure
As fiery storms, ablaze with thund'rous howl,
Had stirr'd the serpent terrors on their prowl,
To frolic where our dreams and fears endure.
The welkin reddened too with bloody gore
And carmine light reveal'd a scene afoul:
A worldly wound had bled with titan growl
And seismic quakes had rent a bleeding shore.

And out from all the scarring planet's skin
There came the fiery head of Mother-Snake;
Her fangs were rows of deadly pikes within
The mouth of hemlock trees and acid lake;
She expell'd caustic clouds of putrid breath
And devour'd all—a starless void of death.

If Closets Talked

Maxwell I. Gold

Toward the bottom of some radiant place, the Mirrored Ones were there, waiting on the other side of nothing. Dismissive and cruel, their stringy bodies danced across my eyes like the waning visions from my decayed brain. These creatures, misanthropes who dwelled in closets and cellars, were sequestered beneath a dark faceless pragmatism belched in mothballs and mutilation.

Oh, the things they could say.

Trembling, I glared into the arduous black where, at the end of the hall, the Mirrored Ones, they waited. Their wide, hungry mouths yawned into jagged fields of splintered wood, rusty bones, and dried blood. Still, I did my best to ignore them. And why did I feel as if I'd been here before? This place out of a dream, a closet inside my head cloistered beneath flesh and feral judgment concealing the monstrous reflections of my life. The Mirrored Ones groaned, their impatience apparent, while imperfect nails clawed in silence at my feet.

The things they could say.

There was nowhere for me to run, only to confront the endless ruin and fear below me.

Take Out

Jay Hardy

At the diner
They rarely spoke
Unless it was
To share a joke.

She waited tables.
He slung hash.
They both needed
The extra cash.

Until one night,
Death walked in
Wearing his usual
Shit-eating grin.

They recognized
Him on sight.
Death's disguise
Is rarely right.

He didn't order.
Just simply sat.
Death looks trim.
He's never fat.

"Time to go,"
Death told her,
His low voice
A silky purr.

"Take me too,"
The cook said.
"Without her here
I'd feel dead."

The waitress smiled.
Took his hand.
Death got more
Then he'd planned.

They disappeared
Before the fire.
Death didn't trust
A frayed wire.

Sometimes love
Can arrive late,
But it's always
Worth the wait.

Cassilda's Song

DJ Tyrer

Words of song end
With "In Carcosa"
But, the images continue
Dreamlike past my mind's eye
Cloud waves and twin suns
Long shadows and soaring cities
Stars dark instead of bright
Towers rising higher than the moons
And, then, it all vanishes
Gone—just the mundane world
Banal and pointless
Until I play it again
Until I finally dare
To take the final leap
Tear off my earthly mask
Fly down past stars, moons, towers
To settle there, a stranger no more
But, home where I belong
In Carcosa . . .

What Evil Lurks

Adele Gardner

True hearts can still love darkness,
Heeding the rattling skeleton behind the door,
Emerging by night to haunt our dreams.

Still, evil lurks under floorboards,
Houses haunted for a reason, seldom good,
Although ghost hunters relish proof—
Doomed souls still walk, pass messages—
Outing murderers to unearthly detectives
Who solve them by dint of their own darkness.

Andrea in Wonderland

Andrew White

A gothic girl in a place so weird—
Nothing too strange about that!
Look at that creature with a long beard,
And who is that nut in a hat?

Is that the moon calling your name,
Or is it the dragon's voice?
Stuck inside of a chess game—
Is the next move really your choice?

You never know where the trail may lead,
You might reach the Queen's domain.
Watch out for things that are ready to feed
And tea that may damage your brain!

Just keep yourself from getting uptight,
Breathe in that Wonderland air.
The purple sun will shine its light
As you frolic with the hare.

The caterpillar will open his stash
But it's better not to partake.
You might end up as heavenly hash
On top of a Cheshire's cake!

The question is this, is it all in her mind,
Actual events or a dreamlike display?
Her imagination is so refined,
She lives in wonder every day.

"Real" or not, there are worlds to see,
And Andrea loves to roam.
Her mind is open, her spirit is free—
Everywhere she is at home.

Changing Moons

Oliver Smith

Twenty cats at her worn-out, witchy heels.
With twenty cats she is prowling, twitching;
twenty cats in streetlight-shadow weaving.
All following this thing of failing flesh,
of bitter rags, of tattered bones and howling.
To shame her, I named her Mad Miss Catkin.

Up at me her green eye was gazing, from beneath
her wild hair, tangling. Her regard, bright and cold
as moonlight, sultry midnight, magic sparkling
in the pitch-black shadows of the gutter
as she muttered some strange rhyme. Reeling
about her all her cats circled screaming.

Now, at sunset she comes cursing; creeping
as, bright as day, the starlight's burning.
The clock hands slipping, itching at the hour;
the hour of this wayward spirit waking.
A strange furred thing; sinuous and subtle
with hungry eyes. "We are the cat," it cries.

The hairy changeling escaping; clawing its way
from my man-skin, into the hidden house
along secret paths, among the voices of the stars

who whisper, like the flitting silver moth
in waking dreams, and lead me down odd
tracks and trails, across the roof and gables;

among crouching witch-stones; through the crannies,
in the cotes, where grey doves tremble; sleeping.
Up above I sense the barn owl's stealthy hunting
as I steal across the tiles; along the gutters
slink. I stretch a sickle-sharp finger
to scrape the moonlight from the slates.

Lady Cat-thing glares greenly in the garden,
her cat kin pouncing; proudly whiskered
(tails twisting). In the pond, she's reflected
where golden fish are sleeping; where the moon
so sweetly sings; alone in darker water.
In the laurel thicket, where the spider spins,

the cat calls and I follow this seeley-thing,
this witch unequalled, this malkin-queen.
With felted paw, with the velvet precision
of my tongue and claw I perfect the foppish
elegance of my ear and all through this
undomesticated night, shout her praise abroad.

Rabbit Led

Ashley Dioses

My rabbit led me far away from home,
Past alleyways and arches and a dome.
I finally arrived in a new park—
Yet silence fell and there was not a bark.
The owners did not lead or leash their dogs;
Instead, the dogs led them to fields or bogs.
I turned away, still searching for my pet,
But found a hound of white and red upset.
He gazed into my eyes, exploring me;
I reached to touch him, but it would not be.
He barred his teeth, and yet his threat was hollow;
Instead, he turned around and bid me follow.
I knew then that my rabbit was a lure,
And I was in the Otherworld for sure.
He led me past some pillars, rune-carved stone,
Now part of ruins leaves had overblown.
I still pursued my rabbit and had hope
Of finding him, or I could never cope.
I would have to proceed into the wood.
The hound abruptly stopped and there they stood:
A smiling crone and warrior-like youth.
I knew that they, or she, would show a truth.
She was the Morrigan, wise, warm, and old,
Yet he was arrogant if truth be told.
He looked on with disgust and did not want

To clearly be there for his eyes dared taunt.
She spoke in whispers that I did not hear,
Then vanished ere her message was made clear!
The youth still stayed and led me a ways more.
He stopped and pointed toward the distance, for
Ahead was a gazebo gripped with vines.
I squinted hard at it, in search of signs—
I could see nothing through the thickened blooms!
He read my thoughts and yelled, "You should see, womb!"
I woke with such a jolt, his every word
Still fresh, and yet the message still was blurred.
The crone and youth had come to help me grow—
And yet the message, lost, I'll never know.

Lovemaking

Michael Potts

I'm sorry, honey, Ann said. I didn't mean to bite.
Roger grimaced in pain before the grimace turned
to a grin. He lay still, eyes fixed on Ann. She drew
him close, wrapping her arms around him to kiss,
her head moving with his in passion born only
in the best of long-term marriages. She guided
Roger's ear over her heart, and his head bounced
slightly with each beat. After a few minutes
of bliss, she unbuttoned her top and said, Would
you like? Roger grinned in agreement as his head
moved to the place she liked best. The sex
was great, her body shuddering five times.
Ann sighed and replaced the skull near the spine.
She kissed the teeth, already red with her lipstick.
She said, That was the best ever, my darling.
Can't wait until tomorrow morning!

What Do We Believe?

Darrell Schweitzer

What do we really believe,
we hierophants and high priests,
who preside over these lurid and gruesome ceremonies?
Do we believe, as our congregants clearly do
that by the invocation of dark gods,
by the deliberate emulation of evil,
all orgiastic lusts will be gratified
all craving for revenge mollified
all despair and doubt anesthetized
in a reign of chaos and destruction
that leaves no time for thinking?

Do we, who study the ancient books,
speak the blasphemous words aloud,
and perform the unholy rites,
really believe that great and terrible shapes
will rise from the void when we summon them?

Or is it the void itself that seduces,
the promise of a nothingness so profound
that all pain and shame and anger are erased,
all bothersome intellectual inquiry silenced,
in which humankind does not exist and never has
and therefore may be happy?
In this we must believe, though it takes effort.
Even nihilism is an act of faith.

Vestibule of Tomorrow

Adam Amberden

Each breath is slowing,
Yet catching up to the next.
The spiral of Night,
Losing all scale and dimension.
The Shadows hungrily swallowed
That mischievous hand.
The tittering ghost swept away
Untold eons in the sand.

Has a new world begun,
Coldly ruptured space within?
A fleeting glimpse of the past
Darts down dark alleys of my twisted mind.
I strain to see around the corner,
But the light evades my grasping eyes.
Willingly or not, the memory leaps
Into the maw of eternity and dies.

The abyss beckons my name.
"We've taken everything else,
Why not give the rest freely?"
The spiral is gone, the dream is gone.
Echoes of her voice

No longer ring in my ears.
Golden light of The Muse
No longer dries my tears.

What yet remains to give?

Conundrum

Janice Klain

Dim, bright, shadow, light
Searching, gliding, morphing, fright?
Atmospheres changing, shifting,
Hiding just over there in plain sight
Seen, unseen, unidentified—
Are they moving to connect or moving to hide?

Go away, *Go away!* Why are you still there?
Figures appear or were never there
What did we see? what do they fear?
Doing something by doing nothing,
The fog takes shapes, but our senses form falsely.

Why is no one listening? Or should they be responding?
Hark, the herald beings sing, but don't listen too closely
Speaking like words but not making sense of the sounds
Walking . . . yet not talking.

We all see you trying to become one of us,
though not of the same spirit,
Coexisting, sharing realms
Roaming, roaming through dimensions
Known, unknown, we each stay guarded.

Vision of Ys

Wade German

Down, down, through watery deeps
    All shadowy, a soundless peace
    Shrouded the submarine grave
Of ruins shadowed in sleep:
    These were the ruins of Ys,
    Long-ago swallowed by waves:

A kingdom of powers and peace,
    Fallen in thraldom to grave.
    And fathomless dreams of the deep
Were dreams of the city Ys,
    Under that world of the wave,
    Drowned in the kingdom of sleep.

Then voices called from the grave;
    Old Paris sank to the deep,
    Passing through portals of peace,
Whelmed by sea-weedy waves;
    And ghosts rose out of old sleep
    All dreamy with death, from out Ys.

Rising Star

David C. Kopaska-Merkel

Beyond the shallow graves there is a stair,
The rough-hewn risers made for tiny feet,
None but the slenderest of scientists
Can take that road into the unknown depths.

A mile or two below the sunlit world,
The walls are painted with archaic signs,
Strange beasts that rend and trample tiny folk,
And vistas like no scientists have seen.

The stair ends suddenly, vertiginous;
Wind from below; an atavistic scent,
The moan of ninety thousand starving years
Is carried on the Stygian gale;
In ancient days the sacrifices begged
To serve, but these that scream in fear will do.

Rising Star Cave, South Africa, holds the remains of Homo naledi *and the oldest known human culture (~100,000 years old).*

Venom

Arukoya Tarnois

Dress all in black, my love
                 & be my widow
I'll dress in brown
         & be your recluse lover

I know how we can pass the time, I
                 want to see the underside of things
Lay back upon black satin
Show me your red hourglass
Devour me

. . . and we will prove our shadowed vows,
                                     my love
Within these deep refuted dreams
                               of love

The Path

G. O. Clark

Sitting in my
mini English garden,
they pass by one at a time
on our shared path.

A little old man
face timing on his phone,
ignoring his surroundings,
followed by ghosts.

The bent old woman
walking her blind Chihuahua,
her skeleton barely able to
hold her all altogether.

Our mystic neighbor,
her walking stick topped with
a amber colored crystal, spirits
from her past in tow.

The slow parade
continues all day, weather
permitting, and on into the
dark hours of the night,

when the undead
freely wander the paths,
their homes long ago clearing
escrow, new locks in place.

The little old man
changes direction, but little
else, still face timing, his phone
long ago gone dead.

The Dark Seasons

Geoffrey Reiter

I find no constant consolation in
The cycle of the seasons and the stars,
A field of atoms where no man can win.

The cosmos crumbles to the deathly din
Of entropy, where galaxies are scars.
I find no constant consolation in

The empty pitch which darkly threads the thin
Arena for the brutal game of Mars,
A field of atoms where no man can win.

Where is the wonder in that spark and spin
When each lone quark against the space-time spars?
I find no constant consolation in

The vacant stare, the grim and ghastly grin
Of all who fall within the vast void's wars,
A field of atoms where no man can win.

In winter, summer, spring, or fall, the sin-
Sick sky collapses into smold'ring chars.
I find no constant consolation in
A field of atoms where no man can win.

Cemetery Dansers

Katherine Kerestman

Caskets, coffins, sarcophagi, tombs, catacombs, ossuaries, graves, crypts, vaults.
Very good, now whirl around, dip, and droop,
Funerals, requiems, memorial services, vigils, tears,
Ghastly, gory, hideous, ghoulicious . . .
Promenade, curtsy, One and a Fleuret, sink and ne'er rise.

Weep and mourn, tear your hair and gnash your teeth, black jet, linen winding cloths,
Thrice forward step and then leap down,
Skulls, trochanters, vertebrae, worms, slugs, and beetles,
Shudders, shrieks, howls, screams, and cries . . .
Promenade, curtsy, One and a Fleuret, sink and ne'er rise.

For the *Weird Tales* Poets

Steven Withrow

To sing in speaking tones of doom-dark night
To filigree a page for Farnsworth Wright
Was the fate of those poor laureates of fright.

And critics panned them—or they would have done
Had any read their verses. (Not a one.)
No Mencken turned a Wandrei to a Donne.

Their lines resolved to childish disesteem,
Despite their perfect rhyme in perfect scheme,
When pressed into service for a vulgar theme—

An alien dream, the heads on Easter Isle—
Or were they just too Decadent in style?
Their wastes eclipsed *The Waste Land* by a mile.

Even today, when every goth kid knows
The Cthulhu Mythos exclusively in prose,
We shrink from sonnets, and our silence grows.

The Dying Flower of My Soul

Scott J. Couturier

The dying flower
    of my soul
Dyes a bit blacker
    every day,

Until only its crown,
    withered,
Shows a ghost of
    coronal color.

The dying flower
    of my soul
Perishes into decay,
    desiccate,

Parched to dust by long
    neglect,
Fading to gray & gone
    in no flash,

Beauty unseen save
    by Darkness.

Gossamer Gateways

Frank Coffman

There are places where the thin veil is very frail between the realms.
There are cases beyond the pale. Reason will fail. It overwhelms
What we think "True." When we perceive what we believe "Impossible,"
When come in view *Strange Things* that cleave borders that we've thought
    "Uncrossable,"
Then are we tasked to ask, "What's Real?" when the appeal to Logic fails.
What worlds are masked, yet to reveal what they conceal? Sanity quails!
Gossamer gates weaken and tear, and what's *Out There* often comes
    through!
Odd, altered states, weird wights that glare—of us aware!—come into view.

Such *Borderlands*—many have held near us from eld—are not mere myth.
Shadowy lands—though Reason rebelled—some have beheld. Many a
    wordsmith
In songs and tales show alien lands and foreign strands and zones of
    horror.
Belief prevails. And it demands such *Shadowlands* be accounted for.
    Beyond thin veils lie places odd where few have trod and thence
        returned.
    But when veil fails and *They're* abroad, our mere *Façade of Truth* is
        spurned.

Sor Maria and the Devil, Luzbel

Manuel Arenas

My *enthusiastic response to the 1975 Mexican nunsploitation film* Satanico Pandemonium.

Sor Maria has been noticed, for her purity and piety. She has been noticed too for her healing hands, open heart, godly deeds . . . and comely face. Sor Maria has drawn the eye of the devil, Luzbel. She has seen him lurking in the shadows and peering through the windows. She has even seen him in the cloistral icons, and in the watchful eyes of His sundry familiars. He has appeared to her as a sky-clad man and has visited her in the guise of a sister; seeking confidence . . . and more.

    He has professed His love for her and has proffered to her an apple. He has defiled her body with His touch, and polluted her mind with His foul thoughts. Sor Maria is now plagued by loathsome lusts and cruel urges she cannot rein in and has left a wake of blasphemy and butchery she cannot veil. Sor Maria's corruption has been noticed by the Mother Superior, whom she smote, and by the Holy Inquisition, which she fears. But in return for her fealty, Luzbel has promised to save her from the salvation through purification of the fiery cross. He has made her the new Mother Superior of a convent of energumens, for a flock of sheeple. All of whom she will lead, in His name, to their doom, in Satanic Pandemonium.

A Pestilence of Tongues

Joshua Green

Sickness came without a breath of warning
To a twilight city clouded in fog.
And for some that lived to mourn the morning,
Found that they had been cursed by Yoth-Mthog.

The silence of death pierced even the smog,
Before the tongues came, erupting through pores,
Twirling and lashing and ready to flog
The living that hid behind every door.
Sons held their fathers while tending their sores
As the Worm of Words afflicted their jaws.
It erupted and spread its pallid spores
Through the gaping pit of their broken maws.

When next morning came there were no more words,
Only the cheerful trills of thrilled songbirds.

The Old Gray Mansion

Ngo Binh Anh Khoa

Upon the hill the old Gray Mansion stands,
A sprawling fortress of intemperance
Once steeped in vice, now void of prominence—
A rotten tomb whose shadow plagues the land.
Its cobwebbed floors now seldom welcome any
Live visitors, haunted by a quietude
That sends the bravest to a fretful mood
When they traverse its yawning halls where many
Went missing, never to be found again.
The lucky few that came back lost their minds
And spoke of evil things they'd therein find—
Of eerie murmurs, laughter, shrieks of pain,
And faceless things spewed out by looming shades,
Which chased and bound their prey to that cursed place
Where all trapped souls are severed from God's grace.

Dead Summer

Denise Dumars

In the dead of summer
that we all are about to know
each sad longing crisped and sundered
from the deaths of long ago

When the blackened window opens
and the flame is upon the smoke
thousand-year-old trees perish
our pursuits are but a joke

Why worry of gold or pattern
your life on a foolish plan
when all is about to be shattered
farewell to the heirs of man

As sere summer coughs us out
like breath of a pestilent breeze
no more children play and gambol
they can only choke and wheeze

For this you have traded your future
for this you have lost your past
in all these temporary pleasures
you are about to learn what lasts.

The Messengers

Manuel Pérez-Campos

In raven-borne October, when dead leaves
bring the fall of night into one's hands, for
many a flood-prone serpentine league
of cobblestone the brown waves of the swollen
river regurgitate into a rambling starlit town

the phantasms of last year's drowned: whether
in rags or ungarbed, they lurch with ungainly
effort, as though unable to remember their limbs:
and their touch, whenever detained or embraced
by those who deem themselves a conscience

for the rest, is as unbearably cold as their silence.
Out of charity they venture to take these who
have lost their will to dream into their hearts
and into their domiciles: only to have them
soon thereafter fade unstoppably until

translucent—and just before their forms dissipate
entirely into the heat begin to weep beyond the reach
of solace, each hiding its face in its hands
as though to hide from itself and their hosts
the horror of being eaten into by oblivion.

Warm Fall

Don Webb

After the hottest driest summer on record
Probably the hottest driest ever on this planet
I'm watching the dry brown dusty leaves
I'm hearing them at twilight
Skittering along the asphalt
Almost conquering the other sounds
It isn't polite to notice them
Or acknowledge they will clean up our dry dusty hot mess
As they did on Venus and Mars in their seasons.

The Stench That Lingers Still

Ngo Binh Anh Khoa

I can't wash off the lingering stench of death
Spread from the thing that must have come from Hell,
Which lurked midst tombstones bathed in moonlight pale
Till it emerged and stole my old friend's breath.
We were, by day, two thieves that roamed around
The regions looking for an easy mark
And, by night, two grave-robbers in the dark
Collecting any useful offerings found,
But while we were at work that fateful night,
Some strange growls in the foul air struck our ears
Ere something vaguely humanoid shambled near,
Its severed head held like a lantern; bright
Were its red eyes and fangs. Toward us, it sped,
And I, too scared to save my stunned friend, fled
While his hoarse screams rang, weakened, and went dead.

Sirens

Marge Simon and Mary Turzillo

Sirens are thirsty tonight.
In the brine, they lap you like kits,
coyly pretending to be pretty and helpful.
They suck your tears, your spit, the plasma from your blood.
They reach out tendrils of singing.
You know you need them—
how can you say no?

They work so hard for you,
dragging with the current,
to pull you under,
to kiss you to breathless,
to take your pleasure,
to slap you against the sand.
You can lie there. It's easy.
You will give what they want.
You will bloat in the tide.

When all thirst is satisfied,
the female slaves file out
to tend the bodies awash in the tide.
Sweet and sad, their voices swell in mourning,
that the sailors' journey into the next world
be swift and tempered with kindness,

for all the cruel matter of their passing.
Their bodies are wrapped in clean linen,
buried deep within the island sands.

The Sirens remain silent
until their victims are dispatched,
the last gull with its last morsel,
their slaves again sequestered
in their grotto by the sea.
Once more, those vixens mount the rocks
to play their harps, to weave their spells
into the winds of ill fortune
that speed you luckless sailors by.

The Trumpets

Maxwell I. Gold

In the distant somewhere cradled below dark stars and amethystine skies whose cloudless, frozen bodies coalesced into terrible pits of cold, I shuddered at the cacophonous blasts that grew in the deep. Louder and heavy as if ancient footsteps into a tired earth, a deathful music rumbled through frigid blackness like some black mass haunting me from the darkest moments of time; a reminder of something ineffable and cruel, awoken by those horns, there was no escape, no shelter.

Huddled below, I watched countless thousands clamor with pathetic hopefulness while the cries of dissonant, doomful orchestrations crawled across the horizons singing anthems of blood and metal. A familiar sensation while all around fragile structures swayed in the frantic songs crumbling one after another, their bodies too frail against sounds twisted together in shadow and heat whereupon the fibers themselves cried, *enough is enough.* Static and sand filled my eyes, brain, and body as if my bones fractured under the immense strain of the melody.

My senses were ruptured and I soon fell to my knees, or what remained of them, humbled by the trumpets in that distant somewhere cradled below dark stars and amethystine skies whose cloudless, frozen bodies coalesced into terrible pits of cold, surrounded by everything and nothing until the last notes were played, the resolution of existence.

The Old Fisherman

Joy Yin

Every full moon
Ripples glide through the clear water
Old fisherman's boat creeks through.

His eyes are old
Bitten by the frosts of time
Staring at the moon

There sprouts a silver trail
Between boat and pearly marble
The old fisherman follows it
Up.

Sailing on the moon
He reunites with his lover
Long lost to the cruel stars.

Mocking Delight
(After Bosch)

DJ Tyrer

In the dank bowels of Hell, literally
Demons make sport of the sinners they have caught
They abuse and misuse and also confuse
Take mocking delight

Sinners reliving their sins, eternally
A punishment poetic and ironic
Debasing their victims' former desires, fiends
Take mocking delight

Refining the perfect joke, infernally
Pleasure begetting pain, mingling joy and shame
Demons conducting an orchestra of fools
Take mocking delight

Sinners, in their turn, tortured, creatively
Nuns transform into sows and renounce their vows
Demons laugh as lustful men cower from them
Take mocking delight

Exalt and mock the sinners, concurrently
Giving them free rein from morals to abstain
Twisting their desires till they cry out to God
Take mocking delight

Live a single day in Hell, repeatedly
The exquisite and intricate tortures fade
Till the demons in their victims' banal pain
Take mocking delight

In the dank bowels of Hell, literally
The demons rejoice in the sinners' poor choice
An eternity of torture, in which to
Take mocking delight

A Moonlit Pursuit

Joshua Gage

A chill wind swells the woods with snow
while shadows gambol to and fro
    between the trees,
and as they sniff the air I know
    they're hunting me.

Frothing bellows behowl the moon
out slavering jaws that seem to loom
    from dreams of old,
and if I'm caught they will consume
    my very soul.

With burning lungs, I weave and wend
while branches snag, and roots upend
    my swollen feet,
but if I stop, night's teeth descend
    to swallow me.

During Happy Hour at the Undead Lounge

LindaAnn LoSchiavo

After our breakup, right around sunset,
Dan's never coming home again became
My grief o'clock. Then Undead Lounge opened,
Barmen preparing drinks as carefully
As a blood sacrifice. One happy hour,
A stranger bought a round and winked at me,
Eyes dark as soul-sheen ashes. Sitting down
In his booth with my glass, I extended
My palm. Instead of shaking hands, he kissed
It thoroughly, a white mist shadowing
Us both, until we were inside his house.
That cocktail must have . . . my confusion . . . how . . .
His breath felt hot along my ears and neck,
Kite-stringing my emotions as we flew.
Did I black out? Anointing rain obscured
A cemetery. Fading, he became
Mere ghostly fragments as the sun came up.

A Highland Cairn

Josh Maybrook

Atop a lone and lofty highland peak,
There lies a cairn, a heap of weathered stones,
Assembled there to mark where lies the bones
Of some dread warlord who, in life, did wreak
Such woe that, of his deeds, few dare to speak,
Except in solemn voice and somber tones.
None mourned his passing save the wind that moans,
Forlorn, upon those mountains, bare and bleak.

Old stories warn, "Make not the fool's mistake
Of tearing down what wiser men have built";
For legend has it that those stones were heaped
Upon that spot in bygone days to keep
The fiend, by whom had so much blood been spilt,
Beneath the earth, for fear lest he should wake.

On the Strings of Fear

Norbert Góra

Dread rains over me,
not a drizzle, but cloudburst;
it's just entered
through the mouth
and it's already
freezing the veins.

Now I'm on the strings of fear,
a puppet stuffed with anxiety;
the audience born of darkness
admires the spectacle
in the theatre of dismay.

This body so weak,
my body is sick,
a sailor and a ship for myself
I was once.

Fearful existence—
thrown into the grave
while alive.

Comes the Reaper

Lori R. Lopez

Heed wisely your time, for no season endures.
Memento Mori, a reminder to die,
When Death will drag us from this stage,
Clinging and clawing, however we try
Hanging on—the curtains must fall.

We are raptly observed, from above and below
By the things we do, or fail to perform.
There are eyes in the folds of darkness feared,
Like spotlights gleaming bright and warm . . .
Yet they burn with a stinging chill of frost.

We are judged on acting with little regard
For opinions and feelings, the lives we meet.
From the sky, from the earth is each one viewed;
With as little mercy for our self-conceit.
And the hour draws near of the Phantom's cost.

No clemency owed for not paying his bill.
You were mailed no invoice to state your dues,
And granted no period of grace ere he shows.
With a hollow tread that taps to the blues,
A grim wraith approaches . . . soon all is lost!

His robe cracks like wings, a flurry of crows
As those sinister footfalls creep down the hall.

Your chance to run expired with the knells
When his ominous shadow lurks on the wall,
And regrets loom taller in a journey's exhaust.

A child races free, then the pace grows heavy—
Saddled by pressures; Ambition's firm yoke.
Yet our days won't be judged by material matters,
But the way we have treated the gentlest folk.
There is no retracing old bridges crossed.

Each moment a choice to do better, do worse
Than the moment before and the many gone by.
There is no escaping the burdens we bear
In decisions wasted that still mortify.
Our fate is a coin repeatedly tossed . . .

And eyes keeping score neither blink nor waver,
missing no marks in the tally of souls.
Bide well every act till your seconds are up . . .
An embossed surface lands; the bell of Doom tolls.
Thumping his scythe, comes the Reaper to call.

The Starveling Girl

Steven Withrow

(After Robert Frost's "A Hillside Thaw")

To think, she tried to give the apple back,
The starveling girl! It wasn't politesse
But strength of will that made the girl resist.
(My son would send me to a home for less.)
The waif came begging at my writer's shack,
Clutching an old half-dollar in her fist.
And I, because she looked so frail and small,
Invited her to sit in my rocking chair.
Her name? "Sabine," she said, and that was all.
I gave her a Granny Smith; that's when she balked.
I sliced it on a plate and offered to share,
But still she wouldn't eat, although I talked.
Her clothes were much too large, her shoes unlaced.
She was eight or nine. Her brown bangs hid her eyes.
Something about her kept me from the phone,
From calling protective services. *Erased*
She seemed—X'd out, as when a person dies.
We sat an hour, content; I sat alone.

It took a jolt to wake me. I had slept.
The starveling girl had vanished. In her stead
She'd left her old half-dollar on the chair,
A silver lizard's visage on its head.
(That's all I kept of all that could be kept.)

The salamander's face looked like my son's,
With nothing of his mother's kindness there.
The tail side showed an apple hollowed out
By a fat worm, and several smaller ones
Were intricately embossed around the rim.
Despite the faerie coin, I had no doubt
The onset of dementia best explained
The morning's visitation. On a whim
I scribbled down the ribbing of this rhyme.
The day died in revisions; it had rained.
The girl who wouldn't eat—what was her crime,
To pay back Death her last unsullied dime
And settle her debt one codger at a time!

When the Dead Dance with Us

Darrell Schweitzer

When the dead dance with the living,
they don't do the zombie stomp,
but prefer instead a subtle waltz,
the music so faint it could be just the wind,
their touch so light you'd take it for a chill,
so that when you move and sway
to what seems a mere whimsy,
you might be dancing with one of the dead,
who seek to remember what they once were
and to remind you what you will inevitably become.

Who Knows the End?

Geoffrey Reiter

In the frigid cold abysses where the warm Pacific waters
Lose the light of molten sunrise—here, the slimy sons and daughters
Of the lurkers in the trenches smolder patient in the deeper
Demon regions of the ocean. For the vicious gruesome sleeper
Far beneath the sparkling clarity of blue and burnished currents
Slowly slumbers till the fullness of his ghastly grim endurance
Finds its culminating moment. Then the sediment is stirring,
And the slipp'ry sinful horror rises clouded in the blurring
Of the lower regions' darkness to invade the light of morning.
He'll eclipse the sheen and shining of enlightened day, a warning
Of a wicked will and evil, slimy, scaly gloom occluding
All the lightness and the brightness, buried bleakly by the brooding
Of the elder elegiac terror rising and ascending,
And his brutal dread beginning marks the moment of our ending.

Dr. Frankenstein's Witch-Princess

Arukoya Tomais

With her electric hair
And her gothic toenails
              tattooed black
She's a jolt to behold
Her names have been carved in stone

"I've given you an acrobat's legs"
                    Herr Doktor said
"And a tight Etruscan ass"
But unbeknownst to her creator
She possesses a murderer's heart

So many suture scars
Her flesh is like a migraine's aura
Yet she's a comely horror
A silver-screen superstar

She has a pale corpse's
              enviable complexion
Lips and labia
      cyanotic blue

The Frankenstein Witch-Princess
She makes the monster's reptile spit
She leaves everyone in stitches
We all carry a torch for her
& knock resoundingly tonight
                    upon her castle doors

Autumn

Scott J. Couturier

Autumn attires me in his fiery cloak—
Touches me with a dead lover's cadaverous caress.
Solemn skies, scuds of cloud somber as smoke—
Fairest fruits of harvest amassed & blessed.

Strawman oversees barren furrows strewn
With shorn stalks, & fallen kernels of half-rotten corn—
Crows flock to feed as October's full moon
Shines palely, a face bloodless & forlorn.

On my porch gleams a jack-o'-lantern grin
To ward off witchery, wights, & unhallowed haints—
Halloween sees guisers out, treats to win
Or wicked tricks to non-givers acquaint.

Wonders of crisp air & hoarded store—
Holy gloaming of living's fervent excess.
Winter creeps nigh wearing mortcloth of hoar—
Cold a ghoul hungering for grave's largesse.

Autumn! Swathe me in crimson mourning shroud—
& are not wraiths now mortal realms allowed?
So a specter spins as sonnet praise for unquiet soul & golden bough.

Born Again

Frank Coffman

The body snatchers were paid their extra fee.
The corpse was "quite fresh"—as had been his demand.
Those who'd derided his work . . . soon they would see!
All details had been so exactingly planned.
"The premise of Shelley's book goes against Fate,"
Smythe had argued. "Attempts to reanimate
The dead! Why, Man, it goes against Nature's Laws.
God would fill any experiment with flaws."

"But Galvani made that dead frog's muscle twitch,"
He'd replied. "I feel sure electricity
Will work."
               That and infernal chemicals which
Had been the key!
                    But what he did not foresee
Was the psychopathic killer born again . . .
Or that its "savior" would be the next man slain.

The Hall Between Labyrinths

Joshua Green

My mind was a fog of connected halls.
There were no thoughts of who I'd been above.
The casket, though small, had opened its walls,
To reveal a labyrinth void of all love.

I was not alone—for horrid things of
Astral splendor followed 'round every hedge.
'Twas not until I saw the snowy dove
That I found my way to the labyrinth's edge.

Here she nested her young to feed and fledge.
In this bright hall she let me catch my breath.
But then she dove off from her narrow ledge,
Reminding me that I had welcomed death.

Conceding to her, I entered the maze,
And began to run from the darkling haze.

Classic Reprints

The Were-Wolves

William Wilfred Campbell

They hasten, still they hasten,
    From the even to the dawn;
And their tired eyes gleam and glisten
    Under north skies white and wan.
Each panter in the darkness
    Is a demon-haunted soul,
The shadowy, phantom were-wolves,
    Who circle round the Pole.

Their tongues are crimson flaming,
    Their haunted blue eyes gleam,
And they strain them to the utmost
    O'er frozen lake and stream;
Their cry one note of agony,
    That is neither yelp nor bark,
These panters of the northern waste,
    Who hound them to the dark.

You may hear their hurried breathing,
    You may see their fleeting forms,
At the pallid polar midnight,
    When the north is gathering storms;
When the arctic frosts are flaming,
    And the ice-field thunders roll;

These demon-haunted were-wolves,
    Who circle round the Pole.

They hasten, still they hasten,
    Across the northern night,
Filled with a frighted madness,
    A horror of the light;
Forever and forever,
    Like leaves before the wind,
They leave the wan, white gleaming
    Of the dawning far behind.

Their only peace is darkness,
    Their rest to hasten on
Into the heart of midnight,
    Forever from the dawn.
Across far phantom ice-floes
    The eye of night may mark
These horror-haunted were-wolves
    Who hound them to the dark.

All through this hideous journey,
    They are the souls of men
Who in the far dark-ages
    Made Europe one black fen.
They fled from courts and convents,

    And bound their mortal dust
With demon, wolfish girdles
    Of human hate and lust.

These, who could have been god-like,
    Chose, each a loathsome beast,
Amid the heart's foul graveyards,
    On putrid thoughts to feast;
But the great God who made them
    Gave each a human soul,
And so 'mid night forever
    They circle round the Pole.

A-praying for the blackness,
    A-longing for the night,
For each is doomed forever
    By a horror of the light;
And far in the heart of midnight,
    Where their shadowy flight is hurled,
They feel with pain the dawning
    That creeps in round the world.

Under the northern midnight,
    The white, glint ice upon,
They hasten, still they hasten,
    With their horror of the dawn;

Forever and forever,
    Into the night away
They hasten, still they hasten
    Unto the judgment day.

[From Campbell's *The Dread Voyage* (Toronto: Briggs, 1893). Thanks to Manuel Pérez-Campos for providing the text of this poem.]

The Other Side of a Mirror

Mary Elizabeth Coleridge

I sat before my glass one day,
And conjured up a vision bare,
Unlike the aspects glad and gay,
That ert were found reflected there—
The vision of a woman, wild
With more than womanly despair.

Her hair stood back on either side
A face bereft of loveliness.
It had no envy now to hide
What once no man on earth could guess.
It formed the thorny aureole
Of hard, unsanctified distress.

Her lips were open—not a sound
Came through the parted lines of red,
Whate'er it was, the hideous wound
In silence and in secret bled,
No sigh relieved her speechless woe,
She had no voice to speak her dread.

And in her lurid eyes there shone
The dying flame of life's desire,
Made mad because its hope was gone,
And kindled at the leaping fire

Of jealousy and fierce revenge,
And strength that could not change nor tire.

Shade of a shadow in the glass,
O set the crystal surface free!
Pass—as the fairer visions pass—
Nor ever more return, to be
The ghost of a distracted hour,
That heard me whisper:—"I am she!"

[From Coleridge's *Fancy's Guerdon* (London: Elkin Mathews, 1897).]

Reviews

The "Wyrd" Tradition

Leigh Blackmore

ADAM BOLIVAR. *A Wheel of Ravens: Alliterative Verse in the Old English Style.* Salem, OR: Jackanapes Press, 2023. 130 pp. $15.99 tpb.

Is there a "wyrd" tradition in weird and fantastic verse? By the use of "wyrd," I mean a poetic tradition flowing from traditional historical sources which focusses on fate or personal destiny, derived from Anglo-Saxon history. The "wyrd" is a powerful force which may control the fate (or doom) of individuals and can, perhaps, be seen as the influence of godlike forces on humankind, or alternatively, be seen as the absence of such personified god-forces, in which case the "wyrd" is seen as an ineluctable power which controls people's destinies.

Adam Bolivar's latest book of poetry dances between time-honored tropes and modern fantastic verse, reviving the traditional while celebrating the sensibility of today. It is a concentrated effort to produce a cycle or sequence of verse with roots in Old English and Norse traditions and cultural values, while also utilizing modern verse techniques. Bolivar is working here in the "alliterative verse" tradition, which has its own (fairly stringent) rules of composition. I must confess to being entirely unaware of the tradition of alliterative verse until encountering it with this collection, but it has been used in the past by such poets as the author of *Beowulf*, by old Norse sagas and the Icelandic *Edda*, by Chaucer and by such modern writers as J. R. R. Tolkien and C. S. Lewis. The foreword by scholar Dennis Wilson Wise concisely explicates the historical and mythic background to Bolivar's handsomely illustrated collection. Bolivar's own introduction spells out the poetic strictures to which he has adhered in composing this verse sequence.

The rhythms of alliterative verse conduce to oral memorization, and one can well imagine Bolivar's verses being recited from memory at a pagan festival or around a campfire. Witches, vampires, dragons, elven queens, giants and giant-killers, and other folkloric figures stalk through these rhymeless verses, mingling with the old gods—Frig (Freya), Woden (Odin), Tiw (Thor), and others known and unknown, including Cyndraca. Other poems are rife with ominous cats and ravens. The thrall of swords and warcraft runs like a bloody thread through the poems, and each verse is a rune that demands recitation aloud. Offering the reader an even more interactive way of experiencing verse, some poems here form an internal sequence of "riddles" that must be solved. Let us raise a glass of mead in Hel to Adam Bolivar, worthy of praise for creating a collection at once so redolent of ancient mystery and of modern creativity. If there is a "wyrd" tradition in weird and fantastic verse, this volume is one of its principal harbingers. Recommended.

Cats, Death, and Poetry

S. T. Joshi

MARY TURZILLO. *Your Cat & Other Space Aliens*. Cleveland: Queen Mab's Workhouse, 2018. 105 pp. $15.95 tpb.
MICHAEL POTTS. *Slipknot and Other Dark Poems*. N.p.: Heartsblood Press, 2021. 86 pp. $8.99 tpb.

These books are by two recent contributors to *Spectral Realms*, but both have been writing poetry for some time. Mary Turzillo's first poem was published all the way back in 1976, and she has published a total of eight poetry collections (several in collaboration with Marge Simon), and she has won Nebula and Elgin awards for her poetry and fiction. The current volume was first published in 2007, but it well merits a new edition, for it is a scintillating display of the diversity of genre, theme, and tone that this author has long exhibited in her poetic work.

The title of Turzillo's book should not be taken to suggest that cats—supernatural or extraterrestrial or otherwise—are the focus of this book; but their mystery, remoteness, and seeming aloofness from human concerns are a persistent motif. In "Augmented" we appear to be dealing with a tough New York City cat, who speaks (as does its owner) in pungent dialect: "Wyncha getta job? / Ya so goddam smart now. / What? asks the cat. Operate a computer keyboard / with these teeny tiny paws?" One of the last poems in the book, "Dinosaurs May Be Ancestors of More Than Birds," presents us with the piquant notion of dinosaur cats: "Velocimouser. This quick-witted / swift catosaur captured prey / by silent stalking, then pouncing. / Clever and voracious, it / may have gone extinct because caught off guard / taking naps / after dismembering small mammals." Somehow this extract reminds me of a poem much earlier in the volume, "Hamsters," a brooding rumination on the brevity and fragility of life.

Even if Turzillo's work spans the genres of science fiction, fantasy, and horror, the last-named element is more than a fleeting presence here, as in "Tiptree," which hints at what hideous things may be lurking in your chimney. "The Monster's Mother" is a vibrant evocation of the tragedy-filled life of Mary Shelley and her imperishable literary creation: "It shouldn't surprise us at all / given the scars on her heart / that in her teenage thriller, / the one she pitied the most / was the monster." "Mollusks" ponders the similarities and differences between these invertebrates and our own species: "I'd love to be a mollusk. / Wouldn't you? / What grand stability."

One could quote Turzillo's poems endlessly. She has an uncanny ability to *end* a poem in exactly the right way, with an exquisite little turn of phrase that encapsulates what the entire poem is saying. It should be evident from my quotations that Turzillo writes exclusively in free verse; but she well knows that in choosing this mode of writing she is not indulging in what L. Sprague de Camp called "lazy man's poetry" (although in the hands of far too many *vers librists* it proves to be exactly that). Her lines, luxuriously long or brutally short as the need arises, are more than replete with symbol, metaphor, and simile that carry the poem without the need for formal meter. And her insights into the troubled fate of human beings in a universe they can scarcely comprehend are the intoxicating fuel that drives her work far beyond the limitations of genre.

Michael Potts, although a professor of philosophy at Methodist University in Fayetteville, N.C., is best known as a novelist and poet. He is the author of at least two previous volumes of poetry, one of which (*Hiding from the Reaper*) is explicitly horrific. The current volume does not profess to be exclusively weird, but elements of terror and the supernatural pervade the book from beginning to end. The last stanza of "At the Bell Witch Cave, Adams, Tennessee" hammers this point home: "Fear pulls me away, / and I stumble on the path / outside to run on red clay, / safe at last with open eyes / to the one who haunts / and why. The witch rises / from the dust of old sins."

If Potts has any theme to which he recurs over and over again, it is the awesome and inexplicable presence of death. In "The Web of Belief" he plainly notes "my obsession over death," and "Child Philosopher" elaborates upon the idea: "I think about death, imagine it, quite literally, / as nothing. Not an empty cup, not the mole holes / I tripped in by the garden, but sheer, absolute / emptiness." "Last Breath" tells the harrowing story of the first-person narrator sleeping in a dead relative's bed. In "Ice Cold" a boy dies long before his time, as he "wandered / into his short obituary." But life is not all wine and roses: "Losing Feeling" is a poignant depiction of the meaninglessness of mundane life ("I'm a spore thrown / down a gray slope onto boring / existence, nothing more").

Like Turzillo, Potts can vivify the most evanescent aspects of human life. "Out of Winter's Ruins" is a gorgeous evocation of that season ("From pallid ruins a vital spirit flows— / the scythe of death the shield of life delays"). "Strays" is not a poem about cats (although Potts and his wife have opened their home to eight of them), but apparently about memories—the memories of a girl or woman with "a cancer-eaten brain."

Several poems in this volume are explicitly Christian, but "Hiding" grimly depicts the hell that religious fundamentalists gleefully envision for the rest of us: "The preacher once said / that hell was like a stove / burner turned on high— / *Put your hand on it / and hold it down, / listen to it sizzle.*" But the Christian heaven seems pretty far off in "The Moralist," where death is keenly etched in italics: *"you'll never part / from the sleep of blessed nothingness."*

Readers of *Spectral Realms* should be grateful that two poets whose work has infused such a wealth of meaning into "weird verse" are now gracing its pages.

The Poetry of Youth

Leigh Blackmore

ASHLEY DIOSES. *Darkest Days and Haunted Ways.* Salem, OR: Jackanapes Press, 2023. 102 pp. $13.99 tpb.

Darkest Days and Haunted Ways represents something of a coda to the poet's acclaimed collection *The Withering* (2020). Avowedly the work of a younger poet, it collects material that was not gathered in the earlier volume. Does that make it a lesser work? Perhaps to some degree. Written when the poet was between the ages of fourteen and seventeen, the poems gathered here do not feature as lush a romantic/Gothic framework as some of Dioses's later work, for instance the poems collected in her debut published volume, *Diary of a Sorceress* (2017). One might be tempted to regard them as apprentice efforts.

However, these verses are uniformly visceral and affecting. *Darkest Days and Haunted Ways* is divided into five sections, respectively: "Pulse," "Torn Up Inside," "Wither," "The Wrath Inside," and "Embrace the Darkness." While several of the poems have been published elsewhere, the majority are original to this collection. Dealing with such topics as misery versus happiness, fear, pain, lies, darkness, cold, and death, Dioses dissects her themes with short, sharp lines as keen as a scalpel blade. In a confessional afterword, the poet writes of her father's lifelong illness, and how she sees the structure of this collection as emulating the five stages of grief. Each verse is deeply felt, and if there is the occasional technical infelicity, such as the rhyming of "flutter" with "shudders" ("Forever Lost"), the sheer emotive power inherent in these brief poems of loss and decay cannot help but recall the spare lines of such poets as Baudelaire and Joseph Payne Brennan. Dan Sauer's collage-inspired illustrations depicting skeletonic forms and skulls provide a suitable framework within which the poems jab at the soul of the reader. A *memento mori*, indeed. *Darkest Days and Haunted Ways* not only hints at the mastery of form and themes of the "later" Dioses volumes, but possesses its own elegiac spirit, grappling with the inevitable mortality of us all. Dioses enthusiasts will want this collection. Recommended.

Notes on Contributors

Dmitri Akers is a poet of the weird from Adelaide, South Australia (Kaurna country). For him, the cadaverous rot of Python still fills the air at Delphi; the Musai, too, cannot help but see monsters beneath Parnassus. His poetry and prose have appeared in *Penumbra, So It Goes, Midnight Echo,* and *Spectral Realms,* while he has an essay and review in the *Undergraduate Library* and the *Modernist Review.*

John Thomas Allen's favorite poets are all spooky, whether or not they fit into so-called "genre poetry." There has to be something strange about the stuff to get him interested. New York is one of the great homes of "surreal poetry," and he is now reading Eric Basso's *Catafalques,* hoping his chapbook *Cemetery Tour* finds a publisher. (They really do that—give tours for cemeteries.)

Adam Amberden is a human being currently residing on the planet Earth. Possessed of adequate proficiency in the written form of the English language, he sometimes uses this aptitude to produce poetry reflective of his existential dread. Other human beings have, at times, described him as "weird." This issue contains his first published work.

Manuel Arenas is a writer of verse and prose in the Gothic horror tradition. His work has appeared in various anthologies and journals including *Spectral Realms* and *Penumbra* (both from Hippocampus Press) and *Weird Fiction Quarterly* (Alien Sun Press). He has two collections of prose and poetry, available at Jackanapes Press: *Book of Shadows* (2021) and the soon-to-be-released *The Burning Ember Mission of Helldorado & Other Southwestern Gothic Tales.*

Chelsea Arrington's work can be found in the magazines *The Audient Void, Eternal Haunted Summer, Weird Fiction Quarterly,* the folk horror anthology *A Walk in a Darker Wood,* and elsewhere. She hoards books and art and lives in the Greater Los Angeles Area with her husband and their three children.

David Barker has been writing supernatural fiction and poetry since the 1980s. His latest book is *12 Foot Skeleton Poems*. David's work has appeared in many magazines and anthologies, including *Fungi, Cyäegha, Weird Fiction Review, The Audient Void, Nightmare's Realm, Forbidden Knowledge, Spectral Realms, The Art Mephitic, A Walk in a Darker Wood, A Walk in a City of Shadows, For the Outsider: Poems Inspired by H. P. Lovecraft,* and *Weird Fiction Quarterly*.

Leigh Blackmore horror fiction has appeared in more than sixty magazines from *Avatar* to *Strange Detective Stories*. He has reviewed for journals including *Lovecraft Annual, Shoggoth, Skinned Alive,* and *Dead Reckonings*. His critical essays appear in volumes including Benjamin Szumskyj's *The Man Who Collected Psychos: Critical Essays on Robert Bloch*, Gary William Crawford's *Ramsey Campbell: Critical Essays on the Modern Master of Horror*, Danel Olson's *21st Century Gothic*, and elsewhere. New weird verse has appeared in *Penumbra* and other journals.

Adam Bolivar, a native of Boston now residing in Portland, Oregon, published his weird fiction and poetry in the pages of *Nameless*, the *Lovecraft eZine, Spectral Realms,* and Chaosium's *Steampunk Cthulhu* and *Atomic Age Cthulhu* anthologies. Hippocampus Press published his collections *The Lay of Old Hex* in 2017 and *Ballads for the Witching Hour* in 2022.

G. O. Clark's writing has been published in *Asimov's, Analog, Space & Time, Midnight under the Big Top, Daily SF, HWA Poetry Showcase VII, Speculatief* (BE), and many other publications over the last thirty-plus years. He is the author of fifteen poetry collections, the most recent being *Easy Travel to the Stars* (2020). His third fiction collection, *Aliens and Others*, came out in 2021. He won the Asimov's Readers Award for poetry in 2001 and a Bram Stoker Award finalist for best poetry collection. He is retired and lives in Davis, California, surrounded by books, soothed by music, and enjoying bike ride excursions around town.

William Clunie is an American poet living in Berlin. His work has appeared in *Dreams and Nightmares, Star*Line,* and as a collection from Demain Publishing, *Laws of Discord*. He would like to think his primary influences are Shakespeare, Milton, and Poe. He is married to a German woman named Sandra. They are quite happy together.

Frank Coffman is a retired professor of college English, creative writing, and journalism. He has published speculative poetry and fiction in a variety of journals, magazines, and anthologies. His fourth large collection of speculative verse, *What the Night Brings*, was published in August 2023. A collection of his short fiction, *Maxime Miris: 15 Tales of the Weird, Horrific, and Supernatural*, will be out in early 2024. Writing formal poetry in the *Weird Tales* tradition is his mission.

Scott J. Couturier is a Rhysling Award-nominated poet and prose writer of the weird, liminal, and darkly fantastic. His work has appeared in numerous venues, including *The Audient Void*, *Spectral Realms*, *Tales from the Magician's Skull*, *Space and Time Magazine*, *Cosmic Horror Monthly*, and *Weirdbook*; his collection of weird fiction, *The Box*, is available from Hybrid Sequence Media, while his collection of autumnal & folk horror verse, *I Awaken in October*, is available from Jackanapes Press.

Ashley Dioses is a writer of dark poetry and fiction from southern California. Her debut collection of dark traditional poetry, *Diary of a Sorceress*, was published in 2017 by Hippocampus Press. Jackanapes Press has published two collections of her early works, *The Withering* and *Darkest Days and Haunted Ways*. A new collection, *Diary of a Vampyress*, is forthcoming.

Denise Dumars is a widely published author of poetry, short fiction, and metaphysical nonfiction. She has been nominated for the Rhysling, Dwarf Stars, Elgin, and Pushcart poetry awards. Her chapbook *Cajuns in Space* garnered third place for the Elgin Award. Currently her chapbook *Mars Maundering* is nominated. She lives in L.A.'s beautiful South Bay region, but her heart is in New Orleans.

Melissa Ridley Elmes is a Virginia native currently living in Missouri in an apartment that delightfully approximates a hobbit hole. Her poetry and fiction have appeared in *Star*Line*, *Eye to the Telescope*, *In Parentheses*, *Gyroscope*, *Thimble*, *HeartWood*, and various other print and web venues, and her first collection of poems, *Arthurian Things*, was published by Dark Myth Publications in 2020.

Joshua Gage is an ornery curmudgeon from Cleveland. He currently co-edits the horror poetry journal *Otoroshi Journal* with his life partner, Rowan Beckett. His newest chapbook, *blips on a screen*, is available on Cuttlefish Books. He is a graduate of the Low Residency MFA Program in Creative Writing at Naropa University. He has a penchant for Pendleton shirts, Ethiopian coffee, and any poem strong enough to yank the breath out of his lungs.

Adele Gardner's poetry collection *Halloween Hearts* is available from Jackanapes Press. With poems and stories in *Analog, Clarkesworld, Strange Horizons, Daily Science Fiction*, and more, Adele curated the 2019 SFPA Halloween Poetry Reading and serves as literary executor for father, mentor, and namesake Delbert R. Gardner.

Wade German's most recent full-length poetry collection is *Psalms and Sorceries* (Hippocampus Press, 2022). His first collection, *Dreams from a Black Nebula*, is also available from Hippocampus Press. Other titles include four slim volumes of his selected poems with Portuguese translation: *Incantations, Apparitions, Phantasmagorias*, and the latest, *Chapel of Celluloid* (Raphus Press, 2023).

Maxwell I. Gold is a Jewish-American multiple award-nominated author who writes prose poetry and short stories in cosmic horror and weird fiction with half a decade of writing experience. He is a five-time Rhysling Award nominee and two-time Pushcart Award nominee.

Norbert Góra is a poet and writer from Poland. Many of his horror, science fiction, and romance short stories have been published in his home country. He is also the author of many poems in English-language poetry anthologies around the world.

Joshua Green is an author of weird fiction, fantasy, and science fiction. His work has appeared or is forthcoming in *British Fantasy Society: Horizons, Strange Aeon, Spectral Realms, Penumbra, Calliope Interactive*, and elsewhere. He has three wonderful children and a miniature Australian shepherd named Juni.

Jay Hardy is an artist, editor, and poet from knee deep in the heart of Louisiana's Cajun Country. He is a lifelong fan of "The Alphabet Boys": HPL, REH, ERB, and CAS. His poetry is either weirdly humorous or humorously weird. His poems have appeared in *Ellery Queen's Mystery Magazine* and the *Hyborian Gazette*. He has self-published several poetry collections, including *Always Eleven: Poems Inspired by Stranger Things*, *My Mommy Hates Halloween*, *Living Longmire*, *Cats of Cairo*, and *The Paranoid Pirate*.

S. T. Joshi is the author of *The Weird Tale* (1990), *I Am Providence: The Life and Times of H. P. Lovecraft* (2010), *Unutterable Horror: A History of Supernatural Fiction* (2012), and other critical and biographical works. He has edited the works of H. P. Lovecraft, Ambrose Bierce, Arthur Machen, Lord Dunsany, Algernon Blackwood, and other weird writers.

Katherine Kerestman is the author of *Lethal* (PsychoToxin Press, 2023), *Creepy Cat's Macabre Travels* (WordCrafts Press, 2020), and *Haunted Houses and Other Strange Tales* (Hippocampus Press, 2024), as well as the co-editor (with S. T. Joshi) of *The Weird Cat* (WordCrafts Press, 2023) and *Shunned Houses* (Wordcrafts Press, 2024). Her Lovecraftian and gothic works have been featured in *Black Wings VII*, *Penumbra*, *Journ-E*, *Spectral Realms*, *Illumen*, *Retro-Fan*, *Dissections*, *Off-Course*, *Lovecraftiana* and other discerning publications.

With a background in the arts (non-dark), customer service abd admininistration, travel, and tourism, and education, **Janice Klain** has plenty of experiences to draw from as she journeys through the world of the written word.

David C. Kopaska-Merkel won the 2006 Rhysling Award for best long poem (for a collaboration with Kendall Evans), and edits *Dreams & Nightmares* magazine (since 1986). He has edited *Star*Line* and several *Rhysling* anthologies. His poems have been published in *Asimov's*, *Analog*, *Strange Horizons*, and elsewhere. His latest collection, *Some Disassembly*

Required, winner of the 2023 Elgin Award, was published by Diminuendo Press in 2022.

Lauri Taneli Lassila is a scribe of the unnameable from the border town of Tornio, Finland. Lassila's published literary works include poetry, aphorisms, essays, and speculative fiction. In English, his short story *The Root King* was included in the anthology *Azathoth: Ordo ab Chao*, edited by Aaron J. French and published by JournalStone.

Lori R. Lopez is a quirky author, illustrator, poet, and songwriter who likes to wear hats. Her Gothic-toned and extensive poetry collection *Darkverse: The Shadow Hours* was nominated for the 2018 Elgin Award, while individual poems have been nominated for Rhysling Awards. Stories and verse appear in numerous publications. Other titles include *The Dark Mister Snark, Leery Lane, Odds & Ends, The room at the end of the hall, Cryptic Consequences*, and *An Ill Wind Blows*.

Native New Yorker **LindaAnn LoSchiavo**, a four-time nominee for the Pushcart Prize, has also been nominated for Best of the Net, the Rhysling Award, and Dwarf Stars. Her latest poetry titles are Elgin Award winner *A Route Obscure and Lonely* (Wapshott Press, 2019), *Women Who Were Warned* (Cerasus Poetry, 2022), Firecracker Award, Balcones Poetry Prize, Quill and Ink, Paterson Poetry Prize, and IPPY Award nominee *Messengers of the Macabre* [co-written with David Davies] (Audience Askew, 2022), *Apprenticed to the Night* (UniVerse Press, 2023), and *Felones de Se: Poems about Suicide* (Ukiyoto Publishing, 2023).

Josh Maybrook is a writer, poet, and book collector from New Jersey. His work has appeared, or is forthcoming, in *Fiddler's Green, Grimoire Silvanus, Faunus: The Journal of the Friends of Arthur Machen*, and elsewhere. When he is not writing, he can be found browsing secondhand bookshops or exploring the countryside with his wife, Hannah.

Ngo Binh Anh Khoa is a teacher of English in Ho Chi Minh City, Vietnam. In his free time, he enjoys daydreaming, reading, and occasionally writing poetry for personal entertainment. His speculative poems have appeared in NewMyths.com, *Heroic Fantasy Quarterly*, *The Audient Void*, and other venues.

Manuel Pérez-Campos's poetry has appeared previously in *Spectral Realms* and *Weird Fiction Review*. A collection of his poetry in the key of the weird is in progress; so is a collection of ground-breaking essays on H. P. Lovecraft. He lives in Bayamón, Puerto Rico.

Michael Potts is the author of three novels: *End of Summer, Unpardonable Sin*, and *Obedience*, all published by WordCrafts Press. He also has published three volumes of poetry: *From Field to Thicket* (winner, 2006 Mary Belle Campbell Poetry Book Award, North Carolina Writers Network), *Hiding from the Reaper and Other Horror Poems*, and *Slipknot and Other Dark Poems*. He serves as Professor of Philosophy, Methodist University, Fayetteville, North Carolina.

Carl E. Reed is employed as the showroom manager for a window, siding, and door company just outside Chicago. Former jobs include U.S. marine, long-haul trucker, improvisational actor, cab driver, security guard, bus driver, door-to-door encyclopedia salesman, construction worker, and art show MC. His poetry has been published in the *Iconoclast* and *Spectral Realms*; short stories in *Black Gate* and *newWitch* magazines.

Geoffrey Reiter is Associate Chair of Arts and Sciences and Coordinator of Humanities at Lancaster Bible College. He is also an Associate Editor at the website *Christ and Pop Culture*, where he frequently writes about weird horror and dark fantasy. As a scholar of weird fiction, Reiter has published academic articles on such authors as Arthur Machen, Bram Stoker, and Clark Ashton Smith. His poetry and fiction have previously appeared in *Spectral Realms, Star*Line, Penumbra, ParABnormal, The Mythic Circle*, and *Black Wings VII*. His book *The Lime Kiln and Other Enchanted Spaces: Poems and Tales* will be released by Hippocampus Press in 2025.

Ann K. Schwader lives and writes in Colorado. Her newest collection, Unquiet Stars, is now out from Weird House Press. Two of her earlier collections, *Wild Hunt of the Stars* (Sam's Dot, 2010) and *Dark Energies* (P'rea Press, 2015), were Bram Stoker Award Finalists. In 2018, she received the Science Fiction and Fantasy Poetry Association's Grand Master award. She is also a two-time Rhysling Award winner.

Darrell Schweitzer has been publishing weird or fantastic poetry for decades. Not counting comic verse (e.g., *They Never Found the Head: Poems of Sentiment and Reflection*, 2001) his two previous collections of (mostly weird) verse are *Groping Toward the Light* (2000) and *Ghosts of Past and Future* (2008). Hippocampus Press will issue a new volume of previously uncollected and selected poems, *Dancing Before Azathoth*, in 2025. His most recent story collection is *The Children of Chorazin* (Hippocampus, 2023) and his most recent anthology is *Shadows out of Time* (PS Publishing 2023).

John Shirley won the Bram Stoker Award for his book *Black Butterflies: A Flock on the Dark Side*. His first poetry collection, *The Voice of the Burning House*, has been nominated for the Elgin Award for poetry.

Marge Simon is a writer/poet/illustrator living in Ocala, Florida. A multiple Stoker winner, HWA Lifetime Achievement awardee, and Grand Master of SFPA, her works appear in *Asimov's*, *Daily Science Fiction*, *JoCCA*, *Silver Blade*, *Magazine of F&SF*, and more, as well as anthologies such as *Chiral Mad*, *Qualia Nous*, and *What Remains*.

Claire Smith writes about other worlds: fairy tale, folkloric, mythological, and more. Her work has featured in a number of journals and anthologies, including earlier editions of *Spectral Realms*, *Penumbric Speculative Fiction Magazine*, and *A Frolic of Fairies*. She is currently reading for a Ph.D. in English and Creative Writing at the University of Gloucestershire, specialising in Poetry. She lives in Gloucestershire, UK, with her husband, the writer, Oliver Smith and their very spoilt Tonkinese cat, Ishtar.

Oliver Smith is an artist and writer from Cheltenham, Gloucestershire, UK. His poetry has appeared in *Dreams & Nightmares*, *Eye to the Telescope*, *Illumen*, *Mirror Dance*, *Rivet*, *Spectral Realms*, *Star*Line*, and *Weirdbook*. His collection of stories, *Stars Beneath the Ships*, was published by Ex Occidente Press in 2017, and many of his previously anthologized stories and poems are collected in *Basilisk Soup and Other Fantasies*. Smith is studying for a Ph.D. in Creative Writing.

Mary Turzillo won a 2000 Nebula for "Mars Is No Place for Children." Her poetry collection *Lovers & Killers* won the 2013 Elgin Award for Best Collection. Her collaboration with Marge Simon, *Sweet Poison*, also won an Elgin. Her latest two books are *Cast from Darkness*, also with Simon, and *Cosmic Cats and Fantastic Furballs*. In a Kent State Trumbull production of *Macbeth*, she was the first witch.

DJ Tyrer is the person behind Atlantean Publishing and has been published in *The Rhysling Anthology*, issues of *Cyäegha*, *The Horrorzine*, *Scifaikuest*, *Sirens Call*, *Star*Line*, *Tigershark*, and *The Yellow Zine*. The e-chapbook *One Vision* is available from Tigershark Publishing. *SuperTrump* and *A Wuhan Whodunnit* are available for download from Atlantean Publishing.

Don Webb continues to teach Horror Writing for UCLA Extension, magick classes for University Magickus, and write poetry and short fiction that seem to show up in anthology after anthology.

Andrew White lives like a monk in the mountains of North Carolina. He writes mystical poetry with elements of fantasy, mythology, and Gothic. Andrew loves nature, his family and heavy metal. He has been published in *Spectral Realms*, *Dwarf Stars*, *Kali Yuga Rag*, *Great Tree Zen Temple*, and *Poetry Nation*.

Steven Withrow has written three chapbooks—*The Sun Ships*, *The Bedlam Philharmonic*, and *The Nothing Box*—and a collaborative collection, *The Exorcised Lyric* (with Frank Coffman). His speculative and dark fantasy poems have appeared in *Asimov's*, *Spectral Realms*, *Space & Time*, and *Dreams & Nightmares*. His work was nominated for the Rhysling and Elgin awards, and he wrote the libretto for a chamber opera based on a classic English ghost story. He lives on Cape Cod.

Joy Yin is a writer, poet, and artist from Wuhan, China, though she has lived in California for five years. She is fluent in Mandarin and English but is also learning Spanish. Joy has always had a love for reading and writing. As of now, she has works either forthcoming or already published in *Skipping Stones Magazine*, *Scfaikuest*, the new *Drabbun Anthology* (Hiraeth Books), *Cold Moon Journal*, *Triya*, *Star*Line*, and more.

www.ingramcontent.com/pod-product-compliance
Lightning Source LLC
Chambersburg PA
CBHW060810050426
42449CB00008B/1617